# The Lonely Giant

Written by Lucy Lawrence
Illustrated by Craig Smith

Once upon a time,
as winter was coming on,
an old woman went to live
in a cottage
near the woods.

Nearby there lived a lonely giant.

Every night, the giant
stood outside in the cold
and watched the old woman
through the window.

He could hear
her knitting needles
clicking.

*Clickety clack*

*Clickety clack*

The giant wished that he could
get to know the old woman,
but she didn't even notice him.

4

He felt very puzzled. "After all,"
he said to himself. "I am a giant.
The old woman should be scared of me."

Finally, the giant decided
to give the old woman a fright.

"**That** will make her notice me," he said.

So he suddenly thrust his great head
through the window and shouted,

"Do you see this great **head** of mine?"

But the old woman just
kept on knitting,
*clickety clack, clickety clack.*

"I've seen heads bigger," she said.

The next night, the giant
thrust his great neck
through the window.

"Do you see this great **neck**
of mine?" he shouted.

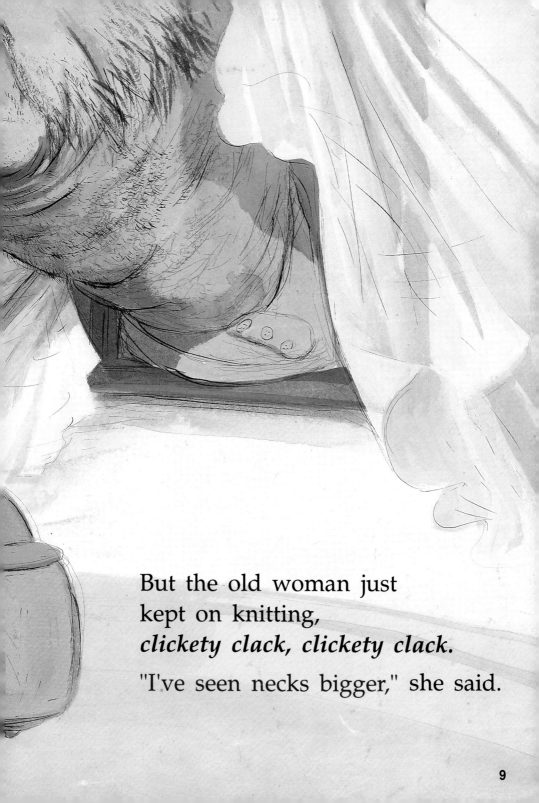

But the old woman just
kept on knitting,
*clickety clack, clickety clack.*

"I've seen necks bigger," she said.

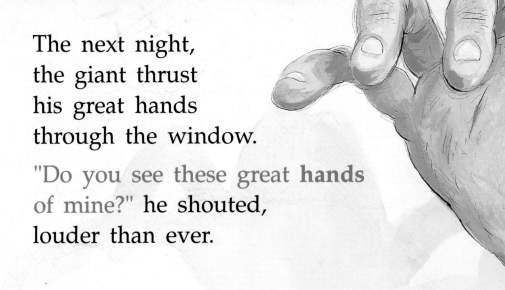

The next night,
the giant thrust
his great hands
through the window.

"Do you see these great **hands**
of mine?" he shouted,
louder than ever.

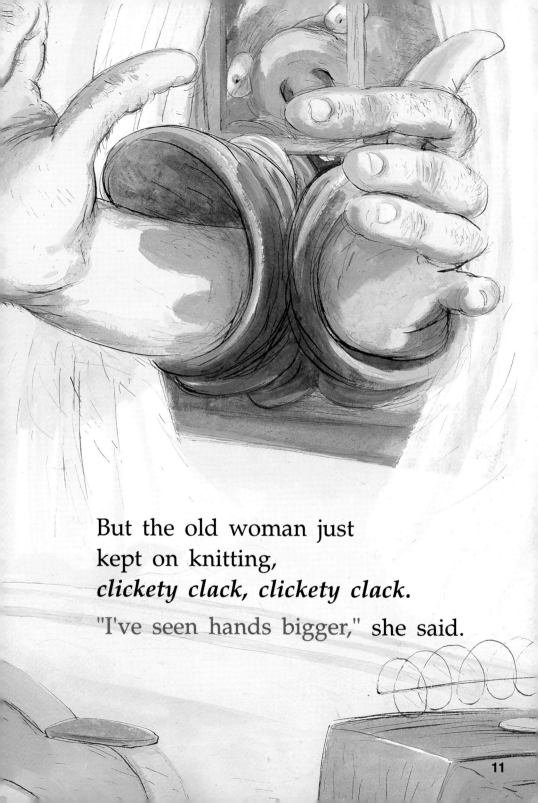

But the old woman just
kept on knitting,
*clickety clack, clickety clack.*

"I've seen hands bigger," she said.

Now the giant roared.

"Well, look at this great foot of mine!
What do you think of **that**?"

13

"I think you are very rude,"
said the old woman.

"Now stop your shouting
and showing off.
I've got work to do!"

The giant did as he was told.
"Sorry," he said,
in a very little voice.

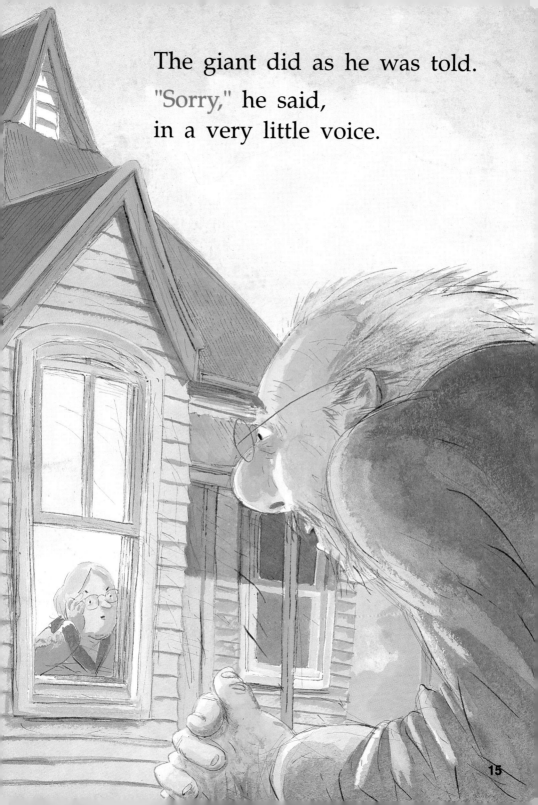

Before long,
*clickety clack, clickety . . .*
the old woman put away
her knitting needles.

"Now **you** have a look
at what **I've** got," she said.
"And let's see if the size is right."

The giant couldn't believe his eyes.

There was a warm woolly hat
for his great big head.

There was a warm woolly scarf
for his great big neck.

There were warm woolly gloves
for his great big hands,

and there were warm woolly socks
for his great big feet.

Suddenly, the giant had an idea.

He ran to the woods
and gathered a great pile of firewood,
big enough to last all winter long.

"Now you can be warm, too," he said.

The old woman smiled.
"Thank you very much," she said.

And before long, a beautiful fire
was blazing.

From that day on,
the old woman and the giant
kept each other company.

"After all," they said,
"that's what friends are for."

And the lonely giant
wasn't lonely any more.